Resumes and Cover Letters for Teachers

Includes:

How to Secure Good References
Advice for Student Teachers
Tips for New Teachers

Dr. Aleathea R. Wiggins

ISBN 0-7414-2375-8

Published by:

PUBLISHING.COM

1094 New DeHaven Street, Suite 100
West Conshohocken, PA 19428-2713
Info@buybooksontheweb.com
www.buybooksontheweb.com
Toll-free (877) BUY BOOK
Local Phone (610) 941-9999
Fax (610) 941-9959

∞

Printed in the United States of America

Printed on Recycled Paper

Published January 2005

To my husband & soul mate
Junghoon Lim

Blessings Always

TABLE OF CONTENTS

Introduction

Resumes and Cover Letters for Teachers is the perfect desktop reference for student teachers, graduates of teacher education programs, individuals seeking a career in teaching, and school administrators. This book contains useful tips for teachers and a variety of sample resumes and cover letters that can be easily tailored to fit the needs of job seekers. Sample reference letters useful for cooperating teachers and administrators that provide letters of recommendation for interns and teachers are also included.

COVER LETTERS
FOR
TEACHERS

Chapter One

Cover Letters for Teachers

Good cover letters lead to job interviews. They make the first impression. They persuade potential employers to read your resume. They are your opportunity to present yourself in the most positive fashion possible. Cover letters should highlight your accomplishments and skills that will enable you to be successful in your chosen profession.

As you advance in your career, or seek to make career changes, your cover letters and resumes become more important. Your cover letter should catch the attention of your readers. It should be written in a professional format, and free of grammar, punctuation and spelling errors. Be sure to keep your letters short and to the point.

Jobs in education, especially for public school teachers, seem to be plentiful these days. Nevertheless, educators need to present themselves in a professional manner. Make a positive first impression by sending a well-written cover letter.

Let's take a look at some sample cover letters for educators.

Dear Dr. Reynolds:

My name is Cynthia Gold and I will graduate from the College of Education at Ohio State University this spring. I am applying for an upper elementary teaching position at Magnolia Park Elementary School.

I completed my student teaching at Magnolia Park Elementary School. In addition to my regular student teaching responsibilities, I developed and taught a six-week science unit. I also organized and directed a class play. My enclosed resume highlights some of my other credentials.

I believe I would fit in well at Magnolia Park Elementary School. I am dedicated and excited about the opportunity to help children develop a love of learning.

I look forward to meeting with you to discuss your goals for the upper elementary positions available at Magnolia Park Elementary School.

Sincerely,

Dear Mrs. Myers:

It has always been my desired to become a teacher and I am dedicated to the field of education. With the enclosed resume, I would like to express my interest in becoming a part of your teaching staff.

I graduated from the University of Idaho with a B.S. Degree in Elementary Education after recently completing my student teaching experience with a class of second grade students.

During my internship, I developed and implemented two teaching units designed to increase students' performance in science and mathematics. These units proved to be effective by facilitating students' interest in science and math while simultaneously enhancing their achievement in these areas.

I look forward to meeting with you to discuss your goals for Silver Creek Elementary School and the contributions that I will be able to make.

Sincerely,

Dear Dr. Santiago:

Are you looking for an enthusiastic and knowledgeable professional to fill the 3rd grade teaching position at Highland Elementary School?

You will see from my enclosed resume that I am the perfect candidate for the position. I recently completed a successful student teaching experience.

During my student teaching experience in an ethnically diverse 3rd grade classroom, I maintained a positive classroom environment and motivated students to learn. I also developed and taught effective, interesting lessons utilizing a variety of teaching techniques.

I am eager to use my strong teaching skills and dedication to the field of education to foster a love of learning in children. I know that I will be able to make a significant contribution to your school. Thank you for your consideration.

Sincerely,

Dear Mr. Jones:

Please take into consideration my request to be considered for the position of 4th grade teacher at Sanford Elementary School.

I recently relocated to Sanford after teaching fourth grade in Atlanta, Georgia for nine years. I have a bachelor's degree in Education from Georgia State University. I qualify for a Florida Teaching Certificate through the reciprocity program.

In my previous position, I served as fourth grade team leader and was an active member of the school improvement committee. Enclosed is my resume, which provides more details of my qualifications and background.

I would like to meet with you to discuss how I will be an asset to Sanford Elementary School. I will contact you within the next few days to arrange a meeting.

Sincerely,

Dear Dr. Snyder:

I was pleased to learn that you have an opening for a music teacher. I have been waiting for the opportunity to help more children develop a love and appreciation for music.

I hold a master's degree in music education from Florida State University. Currently, I am a member of the Florida Symphony Orchestra. I also teach private violin and piano lessons.

I feel that I am the ideal candidate for this position. I would like to arrange a suitable time for us to meet and discuss your goals for this position. I will telephone you next week to arrange a suitable time to meet.

Thank you,

Dear Mrs. Adams:

If you are looking for a behavior specialist for Pearl City High School, you won't find anyone who is more dedicated to young people than I am.

I have been a high school teacher all of my adult life. In my position as a teacher, I've also played the role of a parent and friend by supporting the goals of my students and motivating them to strive for excellence.

I don't just teach science and math. I teach children. I teach them to become better people. I teach them self-respect, how to respect others, and responsibility.

Every Wednesday after school for the past two years, I have volunteered as a tutor at Southern Peak Juvenile Detention Center. I have learned to connect with teenagers in such a way that they want to improve their grades and behavior. I help the students develop a love of learning.

I'd like the opportunity to continue to make a positive difference as a behavior specialist at Pearl City High School. I know that I am the right person for this position. You will read in my resume that I have taken courses in adolescent counseling and behavior management.

I will call you within the next few days to discuss how I can become an asset to your school.

Sincerely,

To Whom It May Concern:

There is nothing more beautiful than the look of excitement on the faces of children as they learn about the world around them.

I believe that it is essential for children to develop a love of learning at an early age. My goal is to provide them with a safe and nurturing classroom environment, conducive to helping them develop into confident and capable learners.

I hold a bachelor's degree in early childhood education and I have several years of experience teaching elementary school. Attached is my resume. It highlights some of my other qualifications.

I look forward to hearing from you.

Sincerely,

Dear Mr. Saban:

Is there anything more important than getting a good education? American children have been falling behind children in other countries in the areas of science and math. For some reason, they don't seem to find these subjects interesting or worthwhile. I'd like to change their perception.

I am certified to teach high school science, biology, chemistry and mathematics. However, I'd like to do more than teach. I'd like to motivate students to explore and investigate the world around them using the knowledge of science and math to do so. I'd like to open their minds to the possibility of becoming future scientists. Science should be exciting and interesting. My goal is to make it that way.

Thus, I was pleased to learn that you are in need of a science teacher at Jones High School. I believe that I am the person you are seeking.

Enclosed is a copy of my resume. I look forward to hearing from you.

Sincerely,

Dear Dr. Goldberg:

Did you know that in most countries outside the United States the citizens are multilingual? As a country, we are weak in foreign language skills. American children will no longer be able to compete in the global market place unless they develop foreign language skills.

Thus, It is essential that we help American students understand the importance of learning a second or even a third language, and develop in interest in doing so.

Please accept this letter as an indication of my interest in the position of Spanish language teacher at Weston Middle School. As you will read on my resume, I speak Spanish, French, and Portuguese fluently.

I'd like to share the wonderful benefits of being multilingual with the students at Weston Middle School as I help them develop proficiency in the Spanish language.

Thanks for your time and consideration. I look forward to hearing from you.

Sincerely,

Dear Ms. Brown:

Nothing is more important than providing children with a good education. The more you know about educational research, the better you will be able to meet the needs of the students you teach.

I understand that you are looking to fill the position of 5th grade alternative education teacher. I recently completed a master's degree in elementary education. My thesis on dropout prevention has allowed me to gain considerable knowledge that will be beneficial in the alternative education program.

Additionally, during my student teaching experience with an alternative education class, I was able to utilize many of the teaching strategies I had researched.

Enclosed is a copy of my resume. I look forward to meeting with you at your earliest convenience.

Sincerely,

Dear Mr. Lee:

Please consider my application for the ESL inclusion teacher position at Los Angeles Central Elementary School. I graduated from the University of California at Berkeley with a Bachelor of Science degree in elementary education and a Master of Science degree in TESOL.

I speak Spanish fluently, and I feel that my experience in learning a second language, along with my education, makes me an ideal candidate for the position.

Enclosed is my resume, which highlights some of my qualifications. I believe that I will be an asset to Los Angeles Central Elementary School.

Thank you for your consideration. I look forward to your reply.

Sincerely,

To Whom It May Concern:

I understand that you are looking for an adjunct instructor to teach English as a second language. My knowledge of second language learning, experience teaching ESOL, and multicultural awareness make me an ideal candidate for the position.

Currently, I work as an ESOL teacher for the Orange County School System here in Central Florida. I hold a professional Florida teaching certificate with the ESOL endorsement, and I have a master's degree in adult education.

Enclosed is my resume that outlines some of my qualifications and background. Please feel free to contact me at your earliest convenience. I look forward to meeting with you to discuss your goals for the position of ESOL instructor.

Sincerely,

Dear Dr. Nelson:

I understand that you are looking for a professor of elementary education to teach in your College of Education.

My 10 years of experience teaching in public schools, four years experience teaching college, and dedication to the field of education make me an ideal candidate for the position. Enclosed is my resume, which highlights some of my qualifications and background.

I would welcome the opportunity to meet with you to discuss your goals for the position of elementary education professor at Ohio State University.

Sincerely,

RESUMES
FOR
TEACHERS

Chapter Two

Resumes for Teachers

Why is your resume important? Your resume is significant because it provides a summary of your qualifications for employment. Good resumes lead to job interviews, which lead to jobs.

Your resume should be easy to read and include essential information such as your career objective, educational background, work experience, accomplishments and special skills. If you speak multiple languages be sure to include this on your resume. Also, include any computer skills that you have.

Your resume should provide the reader with knowledge of your unique personality. Everything on your resume does not necessarily need to relate to the field of education. It is beneficial to present yourself as a well-rounded individual with the ability to work in a diverse setting. You should demonstrate that you are capable of easily adapting to a variety of situations. Life in the classroom is full of surprises. Lesson plans are rarely followed as written. If you plan to begin a successful teaching career, be able to show that you are flexible and able to handle unexpected events.

The person reading your resume will be looking at more than your teaching ability. Do you work well with others? Are you creative? Do you keep up with the latest educational research? Will you be willing to give presentations at teacher conferences and workshops? Do you have time management skills? Are you organized? If so, this should be evident based on your resume.

Resumes are written in various formats. Use whichever format you feel most comfortable with. The style of your resume is less important than the contents. Let's look at some sample resumes.

Michelle Jones
341 Fifth Avenue
Brooklyn, New York 11201
(718) 629-4371

Objective: Seeking a full-time teaching position in an elementary school.

Education: Sarah Lawrence College, Bronxville, New York
                    Bachelor of Science Degree awarded April 2003
                    Major: Elementary Education

Experience: College Park Elementary School, Bronxville, New York
                    Student Teacher from January 2003-April 2003

                    Responsibilities included: developing lesson plans; planning
                    and organizing educational fieldtrips; using the backwards
                    design curriculum; assessing student progress; maintaining
                    student records

Professional
Strengths: *classroom management
                    *progress monitoring
                    *integrating math and science
                    *using cooperative learning techniques

Classroom
Presentation: I facilitated student learning by helping students develop
                    critical thinking skills, promoting positive self-esteem and
                    maintaining a classroom environment conductive to learning

Organizations: Future Educators of America

References: Available upon request

Jennifer Kim
138 Briggs Avenue
Wilton Manors, Florida 33310
(954) 472-6981
E-mail: jkim@hotmail.com

Objective

To secure a position as an upper elementary school teacher.

Education

Bachelor of Science Degree in Elementary Education
Florida Atlantic University, Boca Raton, Florida
Graduated Cum Laude, April 2004

Teaching Experience

Wilton Manors Elementary School - Student Teacher

Responsibilities included:
Working with a diverse student population; Developing and implementing a classroom behavior modification system; Modifying the curriculum to meet the needs of learning disabled and limited English proficiency students; planning and teaching effective, child-center lessons.

Computer Skills

Microsoft Word
Microsoft PowerPoint

Foreign Language Skills

Fluent in Korean

Activities

Girls softball coach
City of Wilton Manors
Summer, 2002 and 2003

References

Available upon request

PHILOSOPY OF EDUCATION

I believe that all children are born with special talents. I believe that as teachers we have a responsibility to help students discover what their special talents are and to nurture those talents. I believe that every child is capable of learning, wants to learn, and wants to grow up to become a productive member of society.

Teachers should keep an open mind. They must try to understand every child in their classrooms. It is important to believe in children and to have high expectations for every child. We as teachers hold the power to the future because the children are the future and they are placed in our hands.

Our classroom environments should always be positive, productive, warm and welcoming. It is essential that the feeling of belongingness exist in our classrooms. Every child under our care and supervision should feel like he belongs, like he is a part of our classroom family. We must teach children to respect each other, to celebrate differences and to realize that they are all special.

As we guide children to be respectful, understanding and considerate of their peers, we need make sure that we give children the same respect as human beings that we expect them to give us. We need to be flexible. We must realize that everyone has different ways of learning and different ways of living. We should vary our teaching styles and use a variety of instructional approaches that address all the different types of learning styles of the children in our classrooms. We must ensure that all children have the opportunity to learn.

Life in the classroom is not about us. It's about the futures of the children and the future of the world that we are shaping through the children. They are very special people and they are put in our care. We have a responsibility to the children and to society to build their self-esteem, provide them with the best possible education that we can give them, and help them develop into life-long learners.

Jamie Williams
2437 North Andrews Street
Fort Lauderdale, Florida 33325
(954) 478-0096

Objective

Position as a TESOL professor in an institution of higher learning

Education

Florida State University
Master of Arts degree in TESOL
Graduation: April 1999

University of Central Florida
Bachelor of Science degree in Elementary Education
Graduation: December 1997

Professional Experience

Lake Eola Elementary School
Fifth grade teacher
August 1999-present

Palm Beach Community College
Adjunct Professor
English for Academic Purposes
August 2000-April 2001

Broward Community college
Adjunct Professor
English as a Second Language
August 1999-July 2000

Leadership

Fifth Grade Team Leader
Teacher of the Year
Teacher Trainer for ESOL
Reading Club Sponsor

Professional Memberships
National Education Association
TESOL

Susan Hill
25 Orange Avenue
Lakehurst, New Jersey 08701
(723) 808-6275

Objective: Position as a middle school English teacher

Professional
Strengths: -Writing and research skills
                      -Presentation and public speaking skills
                      -Working with diverse cultures
                      -Effective in developing and implementing ideas
                      -Developing assessment rubrics

Education: Rutgers University
                      Bachelor of Arts Degree in English
                      Graduated April 2004

Experience: Sunset Park Middle School
                      Student teacher
                      Eighth grade English composition
                      January 2004- April 2004

Activities: Yearbook Club sponsor
                      Poetry writing contest sponsor

Hobbies: Creative writing
                      Avid book reader

References provided upon request

Thomas Bradford
4739 W. Hickory Trail
Charleston, South Carolina 29401
(843) 426-4287
tbrad@yahoo.com

Career Objective   Position as a high school biology teacher

Education   University of South Carolina
                          Bachelor of Science Degree in Science Education
                          Graduated June 2000

Experience   Briggs High School
                          Student teacher 11th grade biology & earth science
                          January 2000- May 2000

                          Responsibilities included:
                          -organizing and managing the science lab
                          -using a hands-on science curriculum
                          -sponsoring the school-wide science fair
                          -writing appropriate lesson plans
                          -developing assessment rubrics
                          -evaluating student progress
                          -integrating science and technology

Computer
Skills   Developing web pages
                          Microsoft PowerPoint
                          Microsoft Word

PHILOSOPHY OF EDUCATION

The education of children should be the most important goal of society. Teachers have a responsibility to help children become independent thinkers and independent learners. Children need to learn how to analyze situations. They need to learn how to use higher-order thinking skills. Children should be actively involved in the learning possess. Teachers should teach them to take responsibility for and participate in their learning experiences.

I believe it is essential that teachers foster a comfortable, child-centered learning environment. I believe that the climate of the classroom is important because the classroom environment affects students' abilities to learn. Teachers should maintain a classroom environment that promotes mutual respect among all children and adults. If the environment is positive, pleasant and organized, students will learn better. I believe that teachers need to work diligently to select teaching topics and assignments that are based on the students' interests. I believe that children learn better when they are interested in what is being taught. Teachers should to be enthusiastic about what they are teaching. When children see the excitement and enthusiasm of the teacher as she is presenting the lesson, it helps to motivate them.

Teachers should be optimists. They should make every effort to maintain a positive attitude and to always look for the good in every situation. Teachers should use kind words in the presence of children. Students need to be disciplined in a positive, respectful manner. Teachers must remember that students should be at the center of the learning process. Teachers need to help students develop a love of learning, to understand the importance of a good education and to help each student to become a better person.

Kelly Goldstein
1427 South 33rd Avenue
Alexandria, Virginia 22301
(703) 774-0963

Objective

Position as an upper elementary school teacher

Education

Howard University
Bachelor of Science Degree in Elementary Education
Minor in Gifted Education
Graduated December 2004

Professional Experience

Bethune Elementary School
Student teacher of 4th grade
September 2004-December 2004

Taught in a multicultural setting using a variety of instructional methods.
Responsibilities included modifying the curriculum to meet the needs of exceptionally gifted students and learning disabled students.

Howard University Tutoring Center
Tutor for basic math and pre-algebra
August 2002-June 2004

Organizations

Future Educators of America
Delta Sigma Theta

Deborah D. Kennedy
4307 W. Banks Road
Chicago, Illinois 60602
(312) 976-4112

Career Objective   To obtain a teaching position in the primary grades.

Education   Florida A & M University
Bachelor of Arts Degree in Elementary Education
Graduated Cum Laude April 2004

Professional Strengths   Public speaking skills
Strong writing skills
Multicultural awareness
Fluent in Spanish and French

**Professional
Experience**   FAMU University School
Student Teacher
January –April 2004

Credentials   Passing scores on the Florida Teacher Certification Exam
(Professional Knowledge/Subject Area/ESOL)

Computer Skills   Training: Technology in Education
Microsoft PowerPoint
Microsoft Word

Activities/Hobbies   Sunday school teacher
Freelance Writer
Avid book reader

Mina Patel
185 Ocean Drive
Tucson, Arizona 85752
(520) 374-2586

Objective: To Secure a position as a middle school English Teacher

Education: Arizona State University
                  Bachelor of Science Degree in English
                  Graduate Summa Cum Laude April 2004

Experience: Jones High School
                  Student teacher
                  Ninth grade English composition and literature

                  Arizona State University Tutoring Lab
                  Peer-tutor for Basic writing skills

Professional
Strengths: Classroom and behavior management
                  Alternative assessment methods
                  Student-centered learning

Memberships: Drama Club
                  Phi Theta Kappa Honor Society
                  Future Educators of America

Computer Skills: MS Word
                  MS Excel
                  MS PowerPoint

References: Available upon request

REFERENCES
AND
LETTERS
OF
RECOMMENDATION

Chapter Three

References and Letters of Recommendation

Plan to secure your references at the beginning of your job search. People such as former college professors, supervising teachers, and co-workers may serve as good references. Before using someone as a reference make sure you have her permission. It could be quite embarrassing for you if a perspective employer calls one of your references and she fails to remember you off hand, or worse, she does not have a favorable opinion about you or your qualifications. Also, it is important to provide your references with a copy of your resume' so they will be well informed of your career goals and be able to speak effectively on your behalf when they do receive calls from your potential employers.

Do not use anyone as a reference if you suspect that he may point out some of your weaknesses or make any negative comments about your character or personality. This does not happen often, but it does happen. You do not want to risk not being offered a position because a bad reference.

One way to ensure that you have good references is to ask for letters of recommendation. If your references agree to write you a letter, I suggest that you offer to write a rough draft of the letter and give them a copy to modify. You know yourself, your background and credentials better than anyone else. Thus, if you draft the letter you can point out your significant achievements, qualifications and career goals. Your reference may not be able to recall these.

Suppose you choose not to draft your own letter of recommendation, and you don't particularly like the one provided by your reference. What will you do then? It is to your benefit to draft the letter yourself.

Let's take a look at a collection of sample reference letters.

To Whom it May Concern:

It is a pleasurable task to write a letter of recommendation for Angela Prescott. She was employed as a peer-tutor under my supervision while attending Rutgers University. During this time, she displayed many positive qualities that would allow her to be successful in her chosen field of endeavor.

Angela was a well-adjusted, self-confident and optimistic student. She served as a positive role model for her peers by demonstrating academic excellence. Angela was well liked by others due to her pleasant personality and interpersonal skills. She was always responsible with her work and diligent in her studies.

Therefore, I highly recommend Angela Prescott as a deserving candidate who will make significant contributions to your institution of learning.

Sincerely,

To Whom It May Concern:

This letter is to recommend Mr. Albert Scott. It was a pleasure to have had Mr. Scott as a graduate student in my behavior management class, and to serve as his academic advisor during his master's degree. His academic work was outstanding. He was diligent in meeting all course requirements and obligations. Mr. Scott's oral presentations were always informative and interesting. He is well informed and highly knowledgeable about a variety of educational issues.

I believe that he will make a significant contribution in the field of education. Therefore, he has my highest recommendation.

Sincerely,

To Whom It May Concern:

It is a pleasure to write this letter of recommendation on behalf of Heather Marie Jones. Ms. Jones interned in my third grade class at Hamilton Elementary School. She has a creative teaching style and knows how to maintain the attention of the students. She took an assertive approach to discipline and fostered a positive classroom environment.

Ms. Jones was well organized. Her lesson plans were well written and carried out effectively. I was impressed by the smoothness of her transitions from one subject area to the next. She also did an excellent job of modifying the curriculum to meet the needs of our limited English-speaking students.

Ms. Jones will be an asset to the field of education. She has my highest recommendation.

Sincerely,

To Whom It May Concern:

It is my professional pleasure to write a letter of recommendation for Shannon Wilcox.

Miss Wilcox is an excellent teacher who is always striving to strengthen and improve the teaching profession. She has a positive attitude and a strong sense of purpose.

Her enthusiasm, innovativeness, and genuine concern for delivering the curriculum is exemplary as evidence by the variety of activities she provided to meet the individual interest of all her students.

Miss Wilcox demonstrates the highest level of professional commitment and competency in her work with students and colleagues. To carry out her professional responsibilities, she gives generously of her valuable time, and her work often extends beyond the school day. She sets high standards for herself and her students.

Miss Wilcox is a model teacher and an asset to the professional field.

To Whom It May Concern:

It is a pleasure to write this reference letter on behalf of Sherry Carter. She has been a third grade teacher at Winston Park Elementary School for two years.

Ms. Carter is a bright and capable teacher. She does an excellent job in presenting lessons. She uses a variety of instructional techniques and a varied curriculum to meet the individual needs of her students. Her pleasant personality and professional manner allow her to interact well with students, parents and her colleagues.

I am sure that you will find Ms. Carter to be a dedicated teacher, and a life-long learner. Therefore, I highly recommend her as a deserving candidate. She will do an outstanding job.

Sincerely,

To Whom It May Concern:

It is my pleasure to provide this recommendation letter for Anna McNair. Ms. McNair is a knowledgeable and talented teacher. She is a positive role model for students and her peers. She seems to bring out the best in her students by building their self-esteem, establishing positive teacher-student relationships and providing motivational classroom lessons.

While employed at St. John's Christian Academy, Anna McNair was an active member of the Parent-Teacher Association and the School Improvement Committee. She also served as the spelling bee coordinator.

It was such a pleasure to have Ms. McNair as part of our faculty. Her positive attitude and dedication to St. John's were certainly appreciated.

Ms. Anna McNair has my highest recommendation.

Sincerely,

To Whom It May Concern:

It was a pleasure to have had Christopher Dupont as a student teacher in my fifth grade class at Chesapeake Elementary School.

Mr. Dupont did an excellent job with classroom organization and behavior management.   His classroom rules, expectations and procedures were well established. He was effective in maintaining a classroom environment conducive to learning. Mr. Dupont was also very creative in presenting his lessons to the students. His lessons were challenging, interesting and fun. Throughout his internship, he used a child-centered approach and incorporated various hands-on activities.

Mr. Dupont is dedicated to the field of education. He is self-motivated and resourceful. He is an outstanding candidate and will be an asset to your school.

Sincerely,

To Whom It May Concern:

It is indeed a pleasure to provide a letter of recommendation for Todd Richardson. He was a fourth grade teacher at Briggs Elementary School.

During his employment at Briggs, Mr. Richardson was a dedicated and effective teacher. He used a variety of instructional strategies and participated in professional growth activities. Mr. Richardson promoted positive relationships with parents, students and peers. He served on the school improvement team and provided leadership in the development of school policies.

Mr. Richardson is an outstanding teacher. He will be an asset to your institution of learning.

Sincerely,

To Whom It May Concern:

It is a pleasure to provide a letter of recommendation for Barbara Adams. She has been a third grade teacher here at Clover Heights Elementary School for three years.

Mrs. Adams has a positive attitude and enjoys working with her students. She is diligent in providing them with the most appropriate learning experiences. In order to build a positive relationship with her students, she makes an effort to understand their backgrounds, interests and needs. She effectively communicates with parents by sending monthly classroom newsletters. Additionally, she invites parents to serve as guest speakers, and participate in classroom learning activities.

Mrs. Adams is actively involved in professional activities. She conducts teacher workshops and attends professional conferences. She views learning as a life-long process.

Therefore, I highly recommend Barbara Adams as a deserving candidate who will make significant contributions to your institution of learning.

Sincerely,

To Whom It May Concern:

It is a pleasurable task to write a letter of recommendation for Regina Garcia. I first met Ms. Garcia when she became a member of the faculty at Crystal Lake Elementary School in 2003. At that time, I was the assistant principal. Ms. Garcia was hired to teach fifth grade.

Ms. Garcia is an excellent educator. She has a genuine interest in meeting the needs of her students. She is creative and often takes the time to develop supplementary curriculum materials. Ms. Garcia is an effective classroom manager. She holds high expectations for her students. As a result, they are well behaved and experience academic success.

Additionally, Ms. Garcia takes every opportunity to further develop her teaching skills by attending teacher workshops, taking college courses, and doing independent research on important educational issues.

Ms. Garcia is extremely dependable, cooperative and resourceful. She will do an excellent job.

Sincerely,

To Whom It May Concern:

It is an enjoyable task to provide a letter of recommendation for Vivian Woods who was a student teacher here at West Park Elementary School. She has a pleasant personality and gets along well with others. Ms. Woods enjoyed her internship experience teaching second grade students. She always had a positive attitude and showed concern and compassion for others.

Ms. Woods was an organized and effective in the classroom. She disciplined the students in a caring manner. Her classroom lessons were well planned, interesting and creative. She was skillful in using educational technology.

I have no hesitancy in recommending Vivian Woods. She is an excellent candidate.

Sincerely,

ADVICE
FOR
STUDENT TEACHERS

Chapter Four

Advice for Student Teachers

Get Off to a Positive Start

As a student teacher it is essential that you start out on the right foot. One of the best ways to accomplish this is to make arrangements to meet with your supervising teacher to learn about her expectations and the climate of the school before the start of your student teaching experience. Ask lots of questions. Find out the rules she expects students to follow in her classroom. Inquire about her teaching style and philosophy of education. What type of person is she? Is she flexible, creative and willing to try new teaching ideas, or is she stuck in the dark ages? Will she expect you to follow her teaching style or will she allow you the freedom to implement your personal style? Have other student teachers interned under her guidance? If so, how many? Knowing the answers to these and similar questions is the key to getting off to a good start.

Document Everything

Go out and purchase a journal or some type of bound notebook to use for documentation. It is important that you keep a running record of your experiences, concerns, notes from conversations with your supervising teacher or university supervisor, and so forth. By documenting everything you will be able to avoid possible misunderstandings. If you feel uneasy about any requests made by your supervising teacher, trust your instinct. Write them down and include the dates. This journal is your record of events for your protection should you happen to need it. It should be kept private. Do not inform your supervising teacher that you are keeping this journal. You will be surprised about the internship nightmares that many student teachers have experienced. Thus, be careful and don't make any assumptions.

While you are student teaching make daily use of your journal. If you ask permission to do some type of special lesson or program you need to document it. If the supervising teacher tells you to do something and you are not sure you should be doing that as an intern you need to document that. Later, when you meet with your university supervisor you need to address that issue in a tactful manner. Do not say that your supervising teacher told you to do such-and-such. Just bring up the topic casually and say, "Is it appropriate for interns to …?" If the university supervisor asks why you raised such a question, or tells you that interns should not be doing such a thing, just respond that one of your 'friends' said she did that when she was a student teacher.

I remember when I first did my student teaching with a third grade class. This was about 14 years ago. During the first week of school, I believe it was the second or third day, my supervising teacher informed me that I would take over completely and teach every subject area beginning immediately until the end of my internship. She did not request that I take over full-time right away. She did not ask how soon I'd like to take over full-time. She informed me in no uncertain terms that I would take over full-time immediately if I intended to successfully complete my internship. She elaborated on her student-teaching experience and noted all the crap she had to endure, and she informed me that I too would now have to pay the piper if I wanted to enter the teaching profession.

It was August. I had not yet observed my supervising teacher present a lesson for each subject, but I was expected to teach all these subjects immediately, full-time until the middle of December. I thought this was a bit much. The routines and rules for the classroom had not been established. The students were not settled in and were not aware of the teacher's expectations. Many of them had been behaving quite inappropriately causing her to change the seating arrangement. How could this woman expect me to take over her class full-time when her classroom organization and behavior management systems were not in place?

Fortunately, I did have a handbook from my university with the guidelines that student teachers and supervising teachers were required to follow. One of the specifications was that I had to begin teaching small groups or a few subjects and then increase my responsibilities each week. I also needed to visit other classes in the school to observe teachers of different grade levels. So, in response to my supervising teacher's demand, I pulled out my student teaching handbook and as nicely as possible pointed out that because of my university's regulations I was not 'allowed' to take over full-time this early in the internship. She responded that she did not agree with the manual and that we would do things differently. Wearing a fake smile, I said I was willing to be flexible. Then I stated that I'd need to check with my university supervisor to get his approval. This was enough to cause her to change her mind and stick with the university's guidelines. After all, she had agreed to follow the university guidelines for student teachers prior to my arrival. By now you must know that my internship was not the best experience of my life. I survived, thanks to God and my journal and so will you.

I cannot overemphasize the importance of keeping a journal during your student-teaching experience.

When you are interning you never know the type of teacher you are interning with unless you just happen to know the person, or they are a friend of your family or something like that. You do not know why you are placed in a certain classroom. There are teachers who request interns and there are teachers who do not want an intern, but their principals require them to have one. Knowing which situation you are coming in to is helpful.

Sometimes interns get placed with teachers who request them. These teachers may be close to burnout. Thus, their reason for requesting an intern is not because they love teaching so much that they want to inspire others by sharing all kinds of wonderful ideas. These teachers may simply be tired and frustrated so they want an intern so that they can have a break while still collecting a paycheck. I hope you don't end up with a supervising teacher like this. I hope that your student teaching experience is a lot more fulfilling and enriching than mine.

I believe that good things always come out of what appear to be bad situations. One of the benefits of having had very little support from my supervising teacher was that I learned to become very resourceful, to work well under pressure, to create excellent lessons and to teach with limited supplies. Sometimes we question why we end up in certain predicaments. There is always a reason. I now know why.

My first teaching job was at an inner-city school. I had a class of thirty-something 5th graders. Most of them were from low-income families. I, too, was low-income because teacher pay was lousy. The school had limited resources. My classroom had limited supplies. None of this mattered. Thanks to my student teaching experience, I did not need an abundance of supplies in order to teach well. I was resourceful. I could create a meaningful lesson from a cornflakes box.

I have enjoyed teaching from then until now and I know I always will.

Request Weekly Evaluations

Your university supervisor and supervising teacher will have standard forms for your periodic evaluations. I recommend that you request additional feedback in the form of short narratives or through some type of questionnaire that you develop. It is essential for you to get as much feedback about your teaching as possible. For example, prior to teaching a math lesson, ask the supervising teacher to note the positive aspects of your lesson presentation and areas that could be improved upon. Ask for feedback on any visuals that you develop for use with your lessons. Ask about student reactions to the lesson. Alert the supervising teacher to your willingness to try some of her ideas and teaching techniques. You want to gather as much information as possible to help you present well-planned, interesting lessons. Requesting additional feedback is also beneficial because you will know how you are progressing throughout your entire student teaching experience and there won't be any surprises later. It would be quite unpleasant to learn at the end of your internship that the supervising teacher thinks you are not ready to teach, or not cut out for the teaching profession. What would you do then? Even if you manage to pass against her wishes you may still face difficulties because most principals will expect you to provide a letter of recommendation from your supervising teacher when you apply for a job. And you certainly don't want to use someone as a reference who won't speak favorably about your ability to teach. Therefore, it is imperative that you know where you stand throughout your internship. Many student teachers failed their internships through no fault of their own. Don't be one of them. Establish good communication with your supervising teacher. Know what she thinks about the job you are doing. Be careful. Document everything!

Network With Other Student Teachers

Your student teaching experience will be one of the greatest challenges you will face. It is helpful to establish a support network with other student teachers. You can provide each other with moral support, encouragement, and teaching ideas. You'll be able to share your joys and frustrations. When things become difficult you won't feel so alone on your journey to becoming a teacher. Additionally, having a network will provide you with the opportunity to build a collection of teaching resources. The network could meet weekly or biweekly in a convenient location away from the school and bring copies of units, lesson plans, and worksheets. These extra resources will be useful during the internship and the first few years of teaching. Make sure that your network has an understanding that everything discussed in the group meetings stays between the group members. You all need a safe haven to express yourselves. It is important to maintain trust among all members of the group.

Display Professionalism

You won't get a second chance to make the first impression. From the moment you enter the classroom you should look and sound like a professional educator. Make sure you are neat, clean and well dressed. Pay attention to your hair care, make-up, and personal hygiene. Use academic language and appropriate vocabulary when speaking. Use standard American English in front of colleagues and students. Be an optimist. Don't spread negativity through your words, facial expressions or body language. You never know who is listening or watching. Have a positive attitude. Be a good listener and effective communicator. If you are having a difficult day excuse yourself to the restroom or take a five minute walk around the school to gather your composure. Don't make the mistake of letting the students or supervising teacher see you lose your cool.

Show that you are dependable. Always arrive early and stay late when necessary. Treat your internship as you would your first real teaching job. Don't be afraid to try new ideas. Make adjustments in your lessons to meet the needs of the students. Seek advice and assistance from reliable sources when you need it. Try to attend professional development workshops available to teachers in your area. Do everything in your power to make the most of your student teaching experience.

TIPS FOR
NEW TEACHERS

Chapter Five

Tips for New Teachers

Congratulations! You've landed your first teaching job. Don't you feel wonderful? Aren't you excited? You are probably a little frightened as well.

As a new teacher you will encounter new challenges daily. It is impossible to be fully prepared for what you will face each day in your classroom, but there are steps you can take to help you survive your first year in the classroom.

Plan Ahead

The first thing you should do upon getting hired is to start planning and never stop. You can never plan too much. Make sure you get in your classroom and begin setting up your room, bulletin boards and seating arrangement well before school starts. You should plan to report to work at least one week prior to teacher planning week for the new school year. Try to accomplish as much of your planning as possible before all the other teachers arrive, and before all the meetings begin.

You may not be able to find out who your students will be or how many you will have, but you can still plan ahead. Put together some basic activities and lessons for the first week. Games to help you and the students learn each other's names are always a good idea. Worksheets, which review skills from the previous grade level, will be helpful during the first week. Photocopy sets of basic math and language arts worksheets, and select several books that are appropriate to read aloud to students. Photocopy some fun sheets to serve as short fillers in case you underestimate the time needed for other activities.

Purchase a large 3-ring binder and dividers to use for documentation on students.

Set up a section for each student and write down any concerns or questions you have pertaining to the students. If you notice any unusual behavior, write it down. Make a note when students fail to submit their homework or have difficulty in a certain subject area. If a student appears not to have any friends indicate this in the binder. You should also include all contact that you have with parents. Anytime you telephone a parent to discuss a concern, list the date and time of your call along with a brief note about the conversation. Before you send a letter to a parent make sure you place a copy of it in your binder. Likewise, when parents contact you keep a record of this. Later, when it is time for parent-teacher conferences, you will have documentation on the children. Furthermore, you may need documentation to show your principal, union representative or attorney if a parent makes a complaint against you. Additionally, keep a personal work journal to document any unusual situations that arise at work and conversations with administrators and fellow teachers. You never know when this might come in handy. Refer to the 'Document Everything' section in the previous chapter.

Become familiar with the rules, regulations and policies of your school and school district and follow them without exception. Take the time to get to know your building administrators and their expectations for teachers. Try to find a master teacher in your school to serve as your mentor or buddy. Do this from the beginning. First impressions make a difference. Effort is always rewarded. Planning ahead is the key to a successful first year teaching experience.

Manage Your Time

One of the biggest complaints of teachers is a lack of time. Teachers lack time for planning, teaching and assessment. Many teachers lack leisure time to enjoy with family and friends because they take work home with them every evening and on the weekends. This may lead to family problems as well as teacher burnout. Planning ahead and learning to manage your time are essential for a balanced life.

As a teacher you need to be organized. You need to have a sequential daily schedule of events for your classroom and back up plans. Put together a couple of substitute folders with enough subject area worksheets and activities to last for a minimum of two days. If you have a personal emergency or need to leave early due to illness you will be prepared.

Do not waste time at work. Teachers often waste a lot of time complaining about students, administrators, district policies and so forth. Don't get stuck listening to co-worker complaints. Close your classroom door, lock it if necessary, during your planning period and get to work. Grade your papers, plan your lessons, or put up your bulletin boards. If you need a break then meditate or nap at your desk. But do not waste your planning time listening to complaints, which will zap your energy and bring your spirits down. You should consider eating lunch in your classroom. You'll be free to plan or relax in peace. A minute of quiet time to oneself is always beneficial.

Make use of school volunteers. Arrange to have a volunteer every Thursday or Friday afternoon and use her to handle time consuming tasks. Volunteers could be used to decorate bulletin boards, photocopy worksheets, or assist struggling students with seatwork. A volunteer could even read stories to the class while you catch up on grading assignments or preparing homework. If you develop an effective plan for using volunteers you will have time to accomplish other classroom goals, and you may eliminate the need to take paperwork home.

Plan group projects and cooperative learning activities. These types of assignments cut down on paperwork leaving you more time for other tasks. Likewise, you could correct papers together as a class letting each student check his work. Moreover, don't spend time doing things that your students could easily do. Set up a system of classroom helpers. Students could be responsible for decorating the bulletin boards, tidying up the classroom, and taking papers to the office. They could be trained to collect and file papers. They could also organize and distribute classroom supplies. If you need short periods of uninterrupted time to complete tasks, implement a daily 20-minute silent reading period or journal writing period. This works well towards the end of the day when you need to prepare homework sheets or notes to send to parents. Additionally, if you are really in a bind for time, show an educational video. This will provide you with an hour or so of uninterrupted time. Simply tackle your paperwork or other tasks while the students watch the video. However, make sure the videos you select are educational and related to the curriculum you are teaching. Do not make a habit of using videos to free up time for tasks. Videos should only be used occasionally for this purpose when you are faced with a deadline or pressing task that has to be completed. Otherwise, videos should be used to enhance student learning based on your curriculum goals and the students' academic needs.

Keep committee memberships to a minimum. Most schools require teachers to serve on committees. When it comes to committees do only what is required. No more and no less. New teachers usually get placed on numerous committees and are often nominated as the chairperson. Don't agree to chair a committee. Don't let committees take over your work time or intrude on your personal time. As a beginning teacher you should spend most of your time and energy getting to know you students, becoming familiar with the curriculum, and maintaining a positive, organized classroom conducive to learning. You need to find yourself and your unique style as an educator. Your effectiveness as a teacher and the academic success of your students' are more important than the contributions you make to school committees.

So, learn to say no to extra tasks. Do not overextend yourself by agreeing to participate in various school functions, or to supervise after school clubs and activities. You will not benefit by becoming overwhelmed during your first year on the job. You will be busy enough keeping up with your teaching responsibilities and classroom management. Wait until you see how well you are able to handle your regular workload before you take on additional tasks. It is certainly easier to acquire additional responsibilities than to back out of ones that you have already committed to.

Managing your time at work will allow you to have more time at home to spend with your loved ones, to pursue personal interests, and to relax and renew. Having a balanced life will enhance your performance in the classroom. When life at work becomes a struggle you will survive because you will have your life at home to look forward to. Manage your time and you will manage your life.

Consider Team-Teaching

There are many benefits to team-teaching, especially for new teachers. In general, team teaching will help you save time, provide you with new ideas and teaching methods, help you to overcome feeling overwhelmed and isolated, provide support for discipline concerns, and help you gain self-confidence.

Let's examine how team-teaching could save you time. First, partner with a teacher who teaches the same grade level as you teach. Each of you would select a subject that you are willing to teach twice. For example, you agree to teach math twice and your partner agrees to teach social studies. The two of you would then arrange a block of time for math and social studies instructions. You would teach math to your class while your partner is teaching social studies to her class. Then you would go to your partner's classroom and teach the same math lesson to her students, and she would teach her social studies lesson to your students. Both of you will have one less subject area to develop lesson plans for and one less subject to teach. You would simply share your math lesson plans with your partner so she could place them in her lesson plan book and you would record her social studies lesson plans in your lesson plan book. Periodically, you should rotate the subjects that you will team-teach so that you will know the curriculum for all subject areas and gain experience teaching all the subjects. Occasionally, you could combine both classes of students to teach your selected subject. Your partner would do likewise. Then both of you would end up with an extra planning period on those days.

Having a partner to team with is also beneficial because you will be able gain new teaching ideas and learn different methods of instruction from your partner. You will have someone to discuss your concerns with. You and your partner will be able to give each other moral support. You won't feel isolated and overwhelmed in your classroom because you will have someone to talk to who really understands the challenges you face in the classroom. Family members and friends often do not understand what teachers deal with on a daily basis. However, your team-teaching partner will know and be able to help you.

Moreover, your students will benefit from the team-teaching process. Observing two teachers working together provides a model for cooperative learning in the classroom. Students will also be exposed to different teaching styles and this will increase their levels of understanding across subject areas.

Maintain Effective Discipline

It is imperative that you establish classroom rules prior to the arrival of your students. Select four or five rules that you will expect all students to follow. Keep the rules simple so that the students will easily be able to remember them. You should also develop a list of consequences for students who violate your classroom rules. Teach your students the rules and reinforce the rules regularly. This is especially important during the first few weeks of school. Practice the rules with your students. Have them recite the rules aloud. Discuss the benefits of having rules and why rules are important. Praise the students for demonstrating appropriate behaviors. Make sure that you are consistent and fair when enforcing your rules. Do not show favoritism. Get to know your students and show them that you care. Your goal should be to gain their trust and respect. Do not go into the classroom attempting to gain their love. You don't need their love to maintain a positive learning environment; you need students to respect you as the authority figure in your classroom. Do not be too nice. Avoid bending the rules. You don't want students to take advantage of your kindness, or to see it as a weakness. You want to provide your students with the best educational experience that you can offer them. This will not be possible if you spend more time on discipline than you do on teaching.

Additionally, you must establish efficient and effective routines and procedures for you classroom. Even if your students are well behaved, you will lose valuable instructional time if students don't know what you expect during transitions. Is there a specific way that they should line up to walk to music class? Must they get permission to leave their seats to sharpen their pencils? How often may they leave the classroom to go to the bathroom? Do you have a classroom helper system? What should students do if they complete independent seatwork before time is up? Know the answers to these questions during planning week and be ready to explain your expectations to the students on the first day of school. Continue to practice your routines until they are automatic. Remember, getting off to a good start sets the foundation for a successful academic year. Good luck.

PORTFOLIOS
FOR
TEACHERS

Chapter Six

Portfolios for Teachers

It is essential for beginning teachers to develop and maintain a professional portfolio. Your portfolio should enhance the accomplishments and skills that are stated in your resume.

In general, your portfolio should include a table of contents so that the reader will know how your portfolio is organized. Your resume, college transcripts, a few sample lesson plans that you've successfully taught and a teaching unit that you designed should follow this. Next, include your personal philosophy of education and be prepared to discuss your philosophy. Which teaching techniques and types of lessons support your philosophy? Is your philosophy supported by the latest educational research?

It is wise to include letters of recommendation from your college professors, university supervisor, and the cooperating or supervising teachers from your student teaching experiences. Make sure the letters are positive and highlight your strengths. Don't include any letter that could lead the interviewer to doubt your ability to be successful as a classroom teacher.

Be sure to include assessment rubrics that you developed and alternative assessment methods that you are skilled at utilizing. Likewise, include photographs of student work from your student teaching experiences, special projects you developed or supervised and learning centers that you created.

Additionally, include awards and certificates of achievement that you received. These could be recognition for community service or volunteer work, as well as education related awards. Include a list of relevant educational workshops that you attended. If you have taken and passed the teacher certification exams you may include the scores.

Finally, prepare a list of questions that you would like to ask during the interview. Although you want a job and you are looking forward to getting hired, it is also important that you are selective about the school you choose to go to. You want to know as much as you can about a school prior to accepting a position. How is the school run? What is the school climate like? How does the chain of command work? What is the average class size? What are the students like? What expectations do the administrators have for the teachers in this school? Is special support available for the students that experience academic challenges or exhibit adjustment difficulties? If so, how are these programs organized?   What type of support, if any, is available for new teachers?

Asking questions will help you make an informed decision about whether to accept or decline a job offer. Choose to work at a school that is right for you.

RECOMMENDED READING

Jones, V. & Jones, L. (2004). *Comprehensive Classroom Management: Creating Communities of Support and Solving Problems, 7th Edition.* Boston: Pearson, Allyn and Bacon.

Shalaway, L. (1989). *Learning to Teach: Not Just for Beginners.* New York: Scholastic, Inc.

Windsor, R. & Rowland, W. (2000). *Employment Strategies for Prospective Teachers: A Guide.* Lisle, Illinois: The Advantage Press.

> *Teachers have the power to change the world by changing the lives of children. Thank you for being brave enough to go out there and make a difference. God bless you.*

If you have questions or comments about this book please contact the author via email at: aleathea@hotmail.com